J B Jemiso
Shepherd, Jodie
Mae Jemison /

34028088404703
BC $5.95   ocn890462738
10/09/15

W9-AJP-372
HARRIS COUN...

Rookie Biographies®

Mae Jemison

by Jodie Shepherd

Content Consultant
Nanci R. Vargus, Ed.D.
Professor Emeritus, University of Indianapolis

Reading Consultant
Jeanne M. Clidas, Ph.D.
Reading Specialist

DISCARD

Children's Press®
An Imprint of Scholastic Inc.
New York Toronto London Auckland Sydney
Mexico City New Delhi Hong Kong
Danbury, Connecticut

Library of Congress Cataloging-in-Publication Data
Shepherd, Jodie.
  Mae Jemison/by Jodie Shepherd ; poem by Jodie Shepherd.
     pages cm. — (Rookie biographies)
  Includes bibliographical references and index.
  Audience: Ages 3-6
  ISBN 978-0-531-20595-2 (library binding: alk. paper) — ISBN 978-0-531-20997-4
(pbk.: alk. paper) 1. Jemison, Mae, 1956—Juvenile literature. 2. African American
women astronauts—Biography—Juvenile literature. 3. Astronauts—United States—
Biography—Juvenile literature. I. Title.

TL789.85.J46S47 2015
629.450092—dc23 [B]   2014035677

No part of this publication may be reproduced in whole or in part, or stored
in a retrieval system, or transmitted in any form or by any means, electronic,
mechanical, photocopying, recording, or otherwise, without written permission
of the publisher. For information regarding permission, write to Scholastic Inc.,
Attention: Permissions Department, 557 Broadway, New York, NY 10012.

Produced by Spooky Cheetah Press
Design by Keith Plechaty

© 2015 by Scholastic Inc.

All rights reserved. Published in 2015 by Children's Press, an imprint of Scholastic Inc.

Printed in China 62

SCHOLASTIC, CHILDREN'S PRESS, ROOKIE BIOGRAPHIES®, and associated logos
are trademarks and/or registered trademarks of Scholastic Inc.

1 2 3 4 5 6 7 8 9 10 R 24 23 22 21 20 19 18 17 16 15

Photographs ©: Alamy Images/Charles O. Cecil: 19; AP Images: 17, 30 top right
(NASA), 27 (Richard Drew), 23; Corbis Images/Roger Ressmeyer: 15; Getty Images:
28 (Brendan Hoffman), 24, 30 top left (Bruce Weaver/AFP), 12 (NASA), 3 top right,
31 center bottom (SSPL); NASA: 8 (KSC), cover, 3 bottom, 4, 11, 20 inset, 31 bottom, 31
top; National Archives and Records Administration: 20 main; Scholastic Inc.: 3 top
left; Science Source: 31 center top;

Map by XNR Productions, Inc.

Table of Contents

Meet Mae Jemison

Mae Jemison was an **astronaut**. She was the first African-American woman to travel into space. The smart and hardworking Jemison is also a dancer, a doctor, a teacher, and an author.

Jemison was born on October 17, 1956, in Decatur, Alabama. When she was three years old, her family moved to Chicago, Illinois.

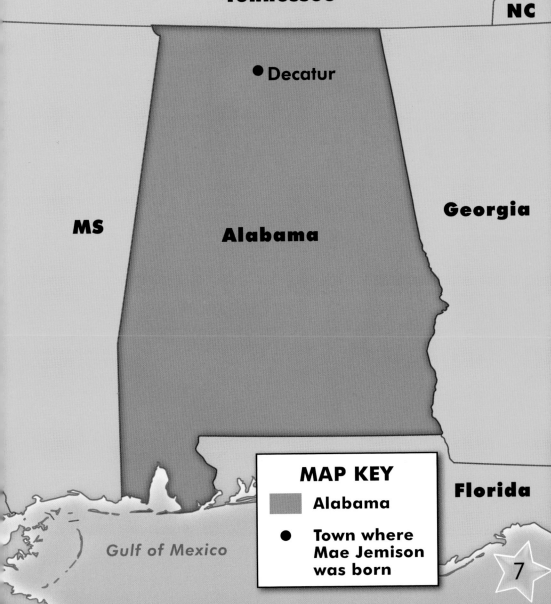

Tennessee

NC

● Decatur

MS

Georgia

Alabama

Florida

Gulf of Mexico

MAP KEY

Alabama

● Town where Mae Jemison was born

Mae Jemison

Jemison learned how to read even before she started school. She was curious about everything. Her kindergarten teacher asked the children what they wanted to be when they grew up. Jemison said, "I want to be a scientist."

Jemison's science background helped her become an astronaut.

Reaching for the Stars

Not many women—or African Americans—were scientists when Jemison was growing up. But young Mae did not let that stop her. She was very interested in **astronomy**. She read books about the stars and the moon. At night, she looked up at the sky and dreamed.

Neil Armstrong and
Buzz Aldrin on the moon

Jemison worked hard and did well in school. Her grades were so good that she even skipped seventh grade. Jemison especially liked to do science experiments.

FAST FACT!

When Jemison was in middle school, Neil Armstrong became the first human to walk on the moon.

Jemison entered Stanford University in California when she was just 16 years old. She was the youngest student in her class. Jemison was still very interested in astronomy and outer space. She watched all the space missions on TV.

In 1981, Americans watched the launch of the space shuttle *Columbia* on TV.

Around the World and Beyond

In 1977, Jemison went to medical school to study to become a doctor. She traveled to Africa and Asia. She took care of people in poor communities.

FAST FACT!

In addition to English, Jemison speaks Japanese, Russian, and Swahili.

In 1983, Jemison joined the Peace Corps as a doctor and returned to Africa. The Peace Corps sends Americans around the world to help improve the lives of people in different countries.

FAST FACT!

The Peace Corps was founded in 1961 by U.S. President John F. Kennedy to help spread peace and friendship around the globe.

A Peace Corps volunteer works with a woman in Africa.

19

Sally Ride

Guion Bluford

In 1985, Jemison returned to California and worked at a hospital. She also applied to the astronaut program at the National Aeronautics and Space Administration (NASA). A year later, she began her training at the Johnson Space Center in Houston, Texas.

FAST FACT!

Sally Ride was the first woman to go into space, in 1983. Later that same year, Guion Bluford became the first African American in space.

Jemison had a lot to learn before she went into space. She learned about the **space shuttle** she would be working on. She got used to moving around in **zero gravity**.

This photo shows Jemison in parachute survival school.

Jemison is ready to board the shuttle.

On September 12, 1992, the space shuttle *Endeavour* lifted into space. Jemison did many experiments on board. Some experiments tested what happened to the human body in zero gravity. The results would help people stay healthy in space.

FAST FACT!

Dr. Jemison was in space for 190 hours, 30 minutes, 23 seconds. That's almost 8 full days!

Jemison left NASA in 1993 and later founded the Jemison Institute. Its mission is to bring technology to poor countries. She also began an international science camp program for teenagers called The Earth We Share.

Timeline of Mae Jemison's Life

1987
accepted into NASA's astronaut program

1956
born on October 17

1992
Endeavour space shuttle launches on September 12

Jemison is also part of a project called 100 Year Starship. Its goal is to help humans travel to the stars in the next 100 years. Jemison is an inspiration to young women everywhere. And she never stops trying new things!

1995
becomes Dartmouth College professor; founds Jemison Institute for Advancing Technology in Developing Countries

2011
joins NASA's 100 Year Starship program

A Poem About Mae Jemison

She dreamed about going to space one day,

then didn't let anyone stand in her way.

Still learning, still dreaming, she makes us say,

"Anything's possible." Hooray for Mae!

You Can Be a Scientist

- Be curious. Always ask, "Why?" and "What if?"

- Work hard to do your best in school and in every area of your life.

- Do not let anyone discourage you. Never stop learning and exploring!

Glossary

astronaut (AS-troh-not): person who travels into space in a spacecraft

astronomy (ah-STRAH-nah-mee): study of space and objects in space (such as the moon and stars)

space shuttle (SPAYS SHUH-tuhl): reusable spacecraft

zero gravity (ZEE-roh GRA-vah-tee): lack of gravity (the force that draws objects to Earth and holds them there), causing objects to float in space

Harris County Public Library
Houston, Texas

Index

Facts for Now

Visit this Scholastic Web site for more information on Mae Jemison:
www.factsfornow.scholastic.com
Enter the keywords **Mae Jemison**

About the Author

Jodie Shepherd, who also writes under the name Leslie Kimmelman, is an award-winning author of dozens of books for children, both fiction and nonfiction. She is a children's book editor, too.

DISCARD

7